THE
MAYANS

Dig Up the Secrets of the Dead

Louise Spilsbury

raintree
a Capstone company — publishers for children

Raintree is an imprint of Capstone Global Library Limited, a company incorporated in England and Wales having its registered office at 264 Banbury Road, Oxford OX2 7DY
– Registered company number: 6695582

www.raintree.co.uk
myorders@raintree.co.uk

Produced for Raintree by Calcium
Edited by Sarah Eason and Jennifer Sanderson
Designed by Paul Myerscough
Picture research by Rachel Blount
Consultant: John Malam
Production by Paul Myerscough
Originated by Calcium Creative Limited © 2016
Printed and bound in China

ISBN 978 1 4747 2686 3
20 19 18 17 16
10 9 8 7 6 5 4 3 2 1

British Library Cataloguing in Publication Data
A full catalogue record for this book is available from the British Library.

Acknowledgements
We would like to thank the following for permission to reproduce photographs: Getty Images pp. 7 (DEA/G. DAGLI ORTI), 23 (De Agostini/Archivio J. Lange), 26 (DEA/G. DAGLI ORTI), 27 (Werner Forman); Shutterstock pp. 1 (Deborah McCague), 4 (Simon Dannhauer), 5 (Leon Rafael), 6 (Sam Chadwick), 9 (Kamira), 10 (Jose Ignacio Soto), 11 (David Pegzlz), 15 (Zimmytws), 16 (Leon Rafael), 17 (Deborah McCague), 19 (Dar1930), 20 (Chao Kusollerschariya), 21 (Howard Sandler), 22 (Ralf Broskvar), 25 (Rudmer Zwerver), 29 (T photography); The Walters Art Museum p. 13 (Gift of John Bourne, 2009); Wikimedia Commons pp. 8 (Leonard G), 12 (AlkaliSoaps/Metropolitan Museum of Art), 14 (Daniel Schwen), 18 (HJPD), 24 (BabelStone), 28 (Förstemann).

Cover photograph reproduced with permission of: Shutterstock: Leon Rafael.

Every effort has been made to contact copyright holders of material reproduced in this book. Any omissions will be rectified in subsequent printings if notice is given to the publisher.

CONTENTS

Throughout the book you will find Deadly
Secrets boxes that show an historical object.
Use the clues and the hint in these boxes to
figure out what the object is or what it was
used for. Then check out the Answer box at the
bottom of the page to see if you are right.

THE ANCIENT MAYANS

The mighty Mayans ruled the forests of **Mesoamerica** (South-east Mexico and Central America) for 1,200 years. The first Mayans were farmers. They lived in small villages near water. They hunted for food in the surrounding swamps and marshes.

Gradually, powerful kings began to control Mayan villages. From around 1000 BC, different kings ruled about 20 separate areas, known as city-states. Each major city had its own king. He ruled the city and the surrounding smaller cities, farms and villages.

Tikal was one of the most important Mayan cities. Up to 100,000 people might have lived here. There would have been farmhouses and fields stretching as far as the eye could see.

Cities of power

At the peak of their power, there were more than 40 Mayan cities, with up to 50,000 or more people crowded into them. The cities were very similar. In the centre, there was always a palace for the ruler. There was also a square or plaza, which was used as a marketplace and meeting place. The centre also had giant pyramids and temples used for worship. The cities became a hub for invention and talent. The Mayans developed a very advanced culture. This included art and building, mathematics and **astronomy**.

The nobles were very important. Commoners could not speak directly to them. To communicate with a noble, a commoner had to speak to a noble's servant. The servant would then pass on the message to the noble.

Secrets of the Dead

Who's who in Mayan society?

In Mayan times, everyone had to know his or her place in society.

- King: He ruled over everyone else in his city-state for life. After he died, the king's son or brother took over.
- Nobles: Relatives of the king were usually nobles. They lived in the central areas of Mayan cities. They were incredibly rich and held the best jobs. They were government officials, army leaders and priests.
- Commoners: The ordinary working people, such as farmers, craftsmen and traders were commoners. Many commoners lived outside the central areas of cities.
- Slaves: The lowest people in all of the Mayan cities were the slaves. They were captured from enemy states. They worked for the kings, nobles and priests.

DIGGING UP THE PAST

Hidden deep in the jungles of Mexico and Central America, the ruins of the Mayan world remained a mystery for centuries. Huge trees had grown up around the ruined cities, hiding them from view.

Since **archaeologists** found the remains of these buildings and the pottery, clay figures, carvings, statues and other **artefacts** buried within them, they have learnt a great deal about the Mayans. Using this evidence, they have worked out how Mayan people lived, their beliefs, who ruled them, what they ate and wore and how they fought.

DEADly Secrets

This is a type of Mayan sculpture called a "stela", or stone tree. These were large stone slabs covered with carvings and writing. The stela usually showed kings wearing huge **headdresses**. They also listed their achievements and the length of their reign. What do you think the stela was for?

Hint: Stone lasts a long time.

This detail is from the 9th century Bonampak murals. It shows a procession of Mayan musicians at court.

Records of a past life

We also know about Mayans from the paintings and written records that they made. The Bonampak **murals** are a series of temple wall paintings. They show scenes from the king's court, war and ceremonies. Mayan writing uses a complicated system of **symbols**. These were carved into stone monuments or pieces of bone, and painted on pottery. They give details about Mayan lives, such as the names of their kings and gods, and details of wars.

Secrets of the Dead

How the Mayans took advantage of nature

- They cut down large areas of trees to clear land for farming and for firewood.
- They cut stone from rocks around them to build homes and temples.
- They burnt trees to heat limestone rock, from which they made lime plaster for building.
- They dug systems of **reservoirs** to hold rain that fell during the rainy seasons. These supplied their cities with enough water.

Answer: The stela was designed to honour a king and make sure his achievements would be remembered. It worked because these stone carvings still tell of the king's successes today.

POWERFUL GODS AND A DARK UNDERWORLD

The ancient Mayans worshipped more than 150 different gods. Most were nature gods, such as gods of the Sun and the Moon. Mayans believed that these gods controlled everything that happened on Earth, from the weather and the harvest to when people were born and whom they married.

Most of the Mayan gods could change forms to look like humans or animals. Each god had a good and an evil side. When events such as droughts, storms and other natural disasters happened, the Mayans believed that the gods were angry with them.

Chaac was the Mayan rain god. Mayans believed he used his lightning axe to strike the clouds and produce thunder and rain.

Death and the underworld

The Mayans believed that the world was divided into the upper world (13 levels of heaven), the middle world (one level: Earth) and the **underworld**. The underworld consisted of nine dark and dangerous levels. Each of these worlds had its own gods. Mayans believed that when someone died, they went to the underworld. There, demons could destroy them. If they got back up through the underworld, middle and upper world, they would reach paradise and eternal happiness.

Five well-known Mayan gods

- Itzamna was the main god. He was lord of the heavens, day and night.
- Chaac was important because he was the god of rain. He watered the **crops**. He was often shown as a sort of dragon with large fangs and big, round eyes.
- Ah Mun was the god of maize, the Mayan's **staple** food. He was always shown as a young god with an ear of maize in his headdress.
- Ah Puch was the god of death. He ruled over the worst of the nine hells in the underworld. He was normally shown with the head of an owl on a human body.
- Ek Chuah was the god of merchants. He was often shown with a spear and sometimes a scorpion's tail.

Priests performed **rituals** and ceremonies to keep the gods happy. Sometimes, the Mayans would **sacrifice** people to ensure the gods would continue to help them.

TOWERING PYRAMIDS
AND HUMAN SACRIFICES

Mayan priests and kings held ceremonies and carried out rituals to keep the gods happy. They believed that to ensure they had good harvests, trade and health, they should offer the gods sacrifices. These were usually animal sacrifices, including iguanas, jaguars and crocodiles.

Sometimes, the Mayans offered human sacrifices. The people who were put to death were often prisoners of war. The Mayans believed that people who were sacrificed went straight to heaven. Sacrifices were made at special ceremonies at the top of high pyramids.

Ceremonies took several days. Music would be played and the victim would be walked around the pyramid base. He or she would be sacrificed on the platform at the top of this pyramid. The priests would hurl the body down the steps.

A second type of sacrifice

Some victims were sacrificed in **sinkholes**. These are deep wells created when underground streams make cave roofs collapse. Archaeologists have found animal and human bones, as well as **jade**, beaded jewellery, pottery and other precious objects in these sinkholes. Mayans may have believed these holes were a way to communicate with the gods of the underworld. They made their sinkhole sacrifices to Chaac, the Mayan god of rain.

DEADly Secrets

Special knives like this one were used in sacrifices. This knife is made from a natural, black, glassy rock called obsidian. Obsidian forms from volcanic lava as it cools. Why do you think Mayans used obsidian to make knives?

Hint: Why should we be careful around broken glass? •••••••

Secrets of the Dead

Why the ancient Mayans built different types of pyramid

- The pyramid used for ceremonies had steps that could be climbed to reach the top. There was a temple and platform there for sacrifices. As priests climbed up the steep steps, they believed that this brought them closer to the gods.
- The other type of pyramid was **sacred**, and not meant to be touched. The steps on these pyramids were too steep to climb without a lot of effort. These pyramids often had doorways leading nowhere. They also had secret tunnels and traps.

Answer: Obsidian is glass-like so it breaks quite easily. When it is carved into a knife, it has an edge much sharper than a normal steel blade.

GOD-KINGS AND BURIAL MASKS

Being a powerful ruler in this life was not enough for Mayan kings. Mayans believed that kings became gods after they died. Kings were buried in elaborate **tombs** filled with treasures, such as pendants made from jade.

Jade is a type of stone. It was more precious to the Mayans than gold. It was believed to be sacred and was used as an **offering** to the gods. Kings were buried wearing jade death masks. This was so that the gods of the underworld would recognize them and treat them as one of their own.

Rulers were buried in jade death masks because jade had religious meaning. Jade was also very valuable so it showed how rich and important a ruler had been in his lifetime.

Tombs at home

When ordinary Mayans died, their family wrapped the body in cotton cloth and buried it beneath the floors of their house. The Mayans believed that this allowed their **ancestors** to watch over them. They also buried the dead person's belongings, and regularly made offerings to him or her. Maize was placed in the corpse's mouth to feed the person on the journey through the underworld. Before burial, relatives painted the remains with a red mineral, called cinnabar, because red was the colour of death.

How Mayans tried to look like gods

The noble families in Mayan times tried to show their connection to the gods by trying to look like them. This resulted in some bizarre body changes.

- In noble families, mothers would hang balls or beads in front of their baby's nose to try to make them cross-eyed. This was in honour of Kinich Ahau, the cross-eyed Sun god.
- Parents would bind their baby's head, especially the sons, so their skulls would grow longer and thinner. Experts think that this was to make their heads become long, like ears of corn, in honour of the god of maize, Ah Mun.

Some Mayans placed their dead (or the bones of the dead) in large urns like this one. The urns were often placed in caves. People then visited the caves to leave offerings. The image on the front of this urn shows what the dead person inside would look like as a god.

CALENDARS AND CALCULATIONS

The Mayans studied the skies from their observatories. They mapped the movements of the Sun, Moon, planets and stars, and used their discoveries to create three calendars.

The Mayans used calendars to plan religious ceremonies, wars and harvests. The Tzolkin calendar lasted 260 days. Each day had a name and number. The Haab calendar was a 365-day calendar like the one used today. However, it had 19 months: 18 with 20 days, and 1 with 5 unlucky days. A special Long Count calendar was used to measure very long periods of time.

From observatories, like the one at Chichén Itzá, Mayans tracked the movement of the planet Venus. They fought their enemies according to where Venus was in the sky.

Mayan maths

The Mayans developed a counting system that was used more than 2,000 years before mathematics was common in Europe. They used the concept of zero more than 1,000 years before any other culture. The Mayans used their counting system for many things, from buying and selling in the market to keeping track of calendar events and predicting solar and lunar **eclipses**.

Secrets of the Dead

The mystery of the Mayan counting system

Instead of counting in tens, the ancient Mayans used a counting system based on 20. This means that instead of counting 1, 10, 100, 1,000 and 10,000, the Mayans used 1, 20, 400, 8,000 and 160,000. Instead of many different numbers, their counting system used just three symbols in several different combinations:

- a dot represented 1
- a bar or stick represented 5
- a shell represented 0.

They used seeds, sticks and shells to do complicated calculations.

Answer: The symbols around the edge represent the names of the months in the Haab calendar.

15

FIERCE WARS AND NEW WEAPONS

The world of the Mayans was not very peaceful. Kings regularly took their armies on violent **raids** against other cities to capture enemies. These hostages were used as slaves and in ritual sacrifices.

Armies also attacked cities to win land or valuable goods. Mayan warriors fought with spears, slings, clubs, axes and knives. They used obsidian to make razor-sharp spear tips. They fired arrows tipped with pointed fish teeth from their bows.

Dressed to kill

Most ordinary Mayan warriors wore very little. They covered themselves in body paint during rituals to prepare themselves for war. Nobles and important warriors often wore long, thick, cotton jackets for protection, and elaborate headdresses. They carried shields that were made from wood or woven reeds. They were covered in animal skin, which could be rolled up and carried on their backs.

Mayan kings were constantly at war with one another.

DEADly Secrets

This ancient carving shows a Mayan warrior with markings on his face. Mayan warriors often had paintings or **tattoos** of animals, such as snakes, eagles or jaguars, on their face and body. Why do you think that was?

Hint: Snakes, eagles and jaguars are very dangerous.

Secrets of the Dead

Mayan tricks and inventions to frighten and defeat enemies

- To show how dangerous he was, a Mayan warrior would often wear a necklace of shrunken heads of previous enemies he had defeated.
- The Mayans invented a type of bomb by filling gourds (large fruits with hard skins) with wasps and bees. They would then throw these at their enemies.
- The Mayans invented a type of **tear gas**. They burnt chilli peppers to create a smoke that they could blow towards the enemy. This smoke stung their enemies' eyes and skin, and made them easier to defeat.

Answer: Warriors used body paint and tattoos of powerful animals to show how important and deadly they were. Some leaders also wore jaguar skins when they went to war. They also filed their teeth into points to add to their ferocious appearance.

17

HARD WORK AND DANGEROUS GAMES

Kings and nobles had slaves to tend to their every need but most Mayans worked very hard. Some worked as builders, stonecutters, architects and porters who carried building materials. Some were artists and others made pots, tools, weapons or statues.

Most commoners were farmers. After harvest, they had to help with building projects. At least once a month, there was a religious festival. There, everyone would feast, sing and dance to worship the many Mayan gods. Sometimes, they would watch a ball game.

The largest ball court ever found is at Chichén Itzá in Mexico. It measured 168 metres (551 feet) long and 70 metres (230 feet) wide.

A game of life and death

Mayan ball games were played on a court shaped like a capital "I". Two teams passed a large rubber ball to each other using only their knees, elbows or hips but never their hands or feet. To score, a team had to get the ball through a stone ring set 9 metres (30 feet) high on the court walls. Crowds came to watch. They bet on Mayan ball games, which were a religious event, too. Kings and priests carried out rituals and music was played. At the end, the winning team might be given trophies and feasts. The losers were sacrificed to the gods.

Ancient Mayan farmers began growing maize (corn) to feed their people in around 2500 BC. This allowed the Mayans to stop moving around to find food and to settle in villages instead.

A farmer's life

The Mayans were skilled farmers. In the spring, to create fields, they cut down and burnt all the trees in an area of forest. They planted seeds in holes, which were made by poking sticks into the ground. To get extra water for crops, they dug canals to carry water from rivers and lakes to their fields. Whole families worked on farms. As well as housework, women helped in the fields to plant crops. Women also worked at harvest time. They took food to markets in baskets balanced on their heads.

RICH TRADERS AND CHOCOLATE MONEY

Jaguar skins, feathers, jade, gold, painted vases, emeralds and other valuable stones are just a few of the items that Mayans traded with each other. They also traded with other people as far away as the Caribbean.

Slaves cleared routes through jungles and swamps, and carried goods long distances in large baskets on their backs. Mayans used large canoes to trade up and down rivers and coasts. Many cities grew bigger and more successful because they were built along trade routes.

These are the ruins of the Mayan city of Tulum. Tulum is unusual because it was built on the coast. It was a seaport, where Mayans traded mainly in turquoise and jade.

Market day

As well as **luxury** goods, Mayan merchants (tradesmen) traded in everyday items, too. These included fruit and vegetables, salt, chilli peppers, vegetable dyes and cooking pots. Farmers brought some food to trade in local markets. Merchants traded other items with each other. They stored goods in large, stone warehouses in cities that became major trade centres. Then the merchants took the goods to city markets to sell. Mayans did not buy goods using money. They gave merchants goods or services in return for the things they wanted to buy.

DEADly Secrets

These are cacao beans. The Mayans used them to make a type of drinking chocolate (see pages 24–25). What else do you think the Mayans used cacao beans for?

Hint: In some places, a slave was said to be worth 100 of them.

Answer: Cacao beans were traded so often that they were sometimes used as a form of money or currency. That just goes to show how much the Mayans loved their chocolate.

Secrets of the Dead

How we know merchants were important and powerful

- In paintings, merchants are usually shown with slaves, sitting on high platforms or being carried from place to place.
- Merchants wore fancy headdresses, carried fans and, sometimes, ceremonial sticks called staffs, which were symbols of importance.
- Merchants had their own god, Ek Chuah, whom they worshipped every day. Ek Chuah is often shown with a spear, suggesting that merchants faced danger on long trips.

FANCY PALACES AND HUMBLE HUTS

Mayan cities were designed to be extravagant. The king's palace was the finest building in town. Palaces were usually built from stone on high ground in the town centre, next to the main square. They were several storeys high. They had colourful, painted murals inside and outside to show how important they were.

There were also courtyards and gardens in the palace grounds, as well as houses where nobles lived. There were buildings and towers where meetings were held. During these meetings, decisions about things such as war, trade and religious festivals were made.

The most famous structure at Kabah is the "Palace of the Masks". The façade is decorated with hundreds of stone masks of the long-nosed rain god, Chaac.

Families at home

Ordinary families lived in a one-room, windowless house. Houses were built around a central courtyard shared with relatives. Rainforests can get a lot of rain in a short time, so houses were built on platforms of stone and earth to raise them off the ground. Walls were made from woven branches covered in clay. The pitched (sloping) roofs were covered in palm leaves. There was a separate hut to cook in and to use as a toilet. Most compounds also had a chicken run and a garden. Inside, people sat on woven mats and slept on hammocks. Only the sons of rich nobles went to school. Farmers' children stayed at home and worked with their parents.

Amazing facts about Palenque Palace

- The palace was built on a 10-metre (33 feet) high platform and covered an area measuring 91 metres (299 feet) high by 73 metres (240 feet) wide.
- It had many rooms arranged around indoor courtyards and halls with vaulted ceilings.
- It had indoor plumbing, a steam bath and two toilets built over an underground stream.
- It had a square four-storey tower that was 25 metres (82 feet) high.
- On the walls there were carved pictures of scenes, such as prisoners being captured in battle, and scenes of Mayan kings and nobles.

These are the well-preserved ruins of Palenque Palace, built in the 7th or 8th century in Chiapas, Mexico.

DRINKING CHOCOLATE AND INSECT SNACKS

One of the things that made the ancient Mayans successful was their ample food supply. Farmers grew fruit and vegetables, including squash, tomatoes and peppers. Their main crop was maize.

Mayans also ate shellfish, such as oysters and clams. They caught fish using nets, harpoons, hooks, and, sometimes, bows and arrows. They used bows and arrows to hunt animals such as **peccary**, deer, dogs and rabbits for meat. One of their greatest inventions was a chocolate drink similar to the hot chocolate people enjoy today.

Magic maize

Maize was a very important crop for the Mayans. They believed that their ancestors were made from maize dough. Maize was full of **nutrients** and easy to grow. They ground the dried maize kernels into a corn flour. This was used to make a paste that could be baked into maize pancakes, known as tortillas. Mayans ate maize porridge or tortillas with most meals.

Ah Mun was the god of maize. Mayans would worship him to ensure that they had a good crop of maize.

DEADly Secrets

Insects were an important source of **protein** because the Mayans had few farm animals. Can you guess their favourite way of eating bugs?

Hint: Eating them this way meant farmers could take them into the fields for lunch.

Secrets of the Dead

How the Mayans made drinking chocolate:

- remove the seeds from cacao pods and let them **ferment**
- dry the seeds in the Sun and then roast them
- remove the shells to get the cacao **nibs**
- grind the nibs into a paste and mix this paste with water
- add spices such as chilli peppers
- pour the mixture back and forth, from cup to pot, until it is frothy
- sweeten the mixture with honey and vanilla. It is now ready to drink.

Answer: Some experts believe tortillas were invented as a way for ancient Mayans to wrap up their bug lunches so that they could take them out to the fields with them.

DRESS TO IMPRESS

What you wear can say a lot about you. Nowhere was this truer than in the land of the Mayans. Royals and nobles took every chance to show off their wealth and importance.

They wore lavish outfits, jade jewellery and clothes made from the skins of jaguars and other dangerous animals. They wore headdresses decorated with beautiful and valuable feathers from rare birds.
They had paintings created of themselves, wearing their finery, on pots and walls.

This Mayan vase has a painting of a noble. He is wearing an extravagant headdress to show how important he is.

Secrets of the Dead

How to tell rich from poor Mayans

- Rich people wore jewellery made from gold, silver, copper, turtle shell and gemstones. Poor people wore jewellery made of bone, sticks or painted clay.
- Royals and nobles wore headdresses – the higher the better. Some headdresses were taller than the people who wore them! Commoners wore cloth turbans on their heads.
- Royals and nobles were the only people allowed to wear feathers in their hair or headdresses. If commoners used feathers, they could be killed.

DEADly Secrets

Only Mayan men could look into obsidian mirrors like this one to see how they looked. Mayans believed it was too dangerous for women to do so. Men looked into a mirror to show how brave they were. Why do you think this was?

Hint: Black mirrors were dark and reminded Mayans of the underworld. • • • • • • • • • • • • •

Colourful clothes

Ordinary Mayan men wore a short skirt. Women wore a long one that wrapped around them. They wore loose shirts made from cotton or from the fibres of a plant called agave. They added colourful layers of fabric belts, sashes and scarves. In winter, they wore ponchos (a rectangular or round cloak with a hole in the middle to put the head through) or cloaks to keep warm. Clothes were dyed using plant dyes. They were **embroidered** with detailed patterns, especially their best clothes, which the Mayans wore on festival days.

Answer: Ancient Mayans believed that monsters from the underworld could grab them and drag them down into the underworld through a mirror.

CRACKING THE CODE

When archaeologists first discovered Mayan **hieroglyphs**, which is their complicated system of writing, they could not work out how it worked or what the symbols meant. After years of hard work, they finally cracked the code.

The Mayan writing system was made up of 800 hieroglyphs. Some showed how to sound out a word. Others are pictures that represented what something means.

A scribe's work

Mayan **scribes** (writers) carved hieroglyphs into stone monuments or pieces of bone, and painted them on pottery and cloth. They also wrote hundreds of books, called codices. These are books of ancient writing that fold up like an accordion. The books reveal many of the secrets about Mayan history, medicine, astronomy and religion.

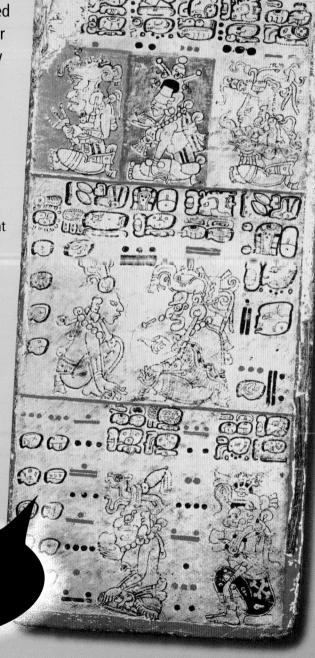

The pages of the codices were made of bark from fig trees covered in white lime. They were bound in jaguar skins.

Hieroglyphs like these were used to record events on Mayan buildings and stone slabs.

Secrets of the Dead

Becoming a scribe

The Mayans knew how powerful words could be, so only the royals and nobles were allowed to learn to read and write and become scribes. A scribe's job was not just to write down what he saw. A scribe's job was to glorify the king and all his deeds. This was to persuade the people and other kings that their ruler was powerful and successful.

The end of the Mayans

One mystery that experts have not yet solved is why the Mayans disappeared. This secret may have been lost when Spanish **missionaries**, who came to the area later, burnt all but four of the codices. What we do know is that by AD 900, the amazing Mayan cities were abandoned and the Mayan **civilization** had collapsed. Experts have many different theories as to what happened. Some think a disease wiped out the Mayans. Others think that they were killed by invaders, struck by a natural disaster or perhaps their habit of burning land for farms made the soil useless for growing crops. No one knows for sure what happened.

GLOSSARY

ancestor relative who has died

archaeologist person who digs up and studies the remains of ancient cultures

artefact object made by a human being that has cultural or religious importance

astronomy scientific study of planets, stars and other objects in space

civilization society, culture and way of life of a particular area

crop plant that is grown for food

eclipse time when the Sun is hidden by the Moon (a solar eclipse) or the Moon is hidden by Earth's shadow (a lunar eclipse)

embroidered decorated with a special type of sewing

ferment split into different substances

headdress elaborate covering worn on the head

hieroglyph special picture of an object representing a word, part of a word or a sound

jade green gemstone

luxury something that is part of living a rich and comfortable life

Mesoamerica region of Mexico and Central America that the Olmecs, Mayans and Aztecs lived in during ancient times

missionary person on a religious mission designed to give help to a particular area

mural wall painting

nibs crushed cacao beans

nutrient substance in food that humans and animals need to be healthy

offering something that is given as part of a religious ritual

peccary pig-like mammal

protein substance found in foods such as meat, eggs and beans that people need to be healthy

raid sudden, surprise attack

reservoir large space where water is collected

ritual action or set of actions done over and over again for a special purpose, often connected to a person's religion or beliefs

sacred something that is important to a religion

sacrifice kill an animal or person to please a god in a religious ceremony

scribe person whose job is reading and writing

sinkhole hole in the ground that forms when soil and rocks above it are washed away by water

staple something that is important because it is used every day

symbol something that represents or stands for something else

tattoo coloured markings on the skin

tear gas gas that irritates and stings the eyes badly

tomb building or space above or below the ground where a dead body is kept

underworld imaginary world of the dead, somewhere beneath Earth

FIND OUT MORE

Books

Daily Life in the Maya Civilization (Daily Life in Ancient Civilizations), Nick Hunter (Raintree, 2016)

Hands-on History! Aztec & Maya: Rediscover The Lost World Of Ancient Central America, With 15 Step-By-Step Projects, Fiona MacDonald (Armadillo Books, 2015)

The Maya and Other American Civilisations (Technology in the Ancient World), Charlie Samuels (Franklin Watts, 2015)

The Maya (Great Civilisations), Tracey Kelly (Franklin Watts, 2015)

Tools and Treasures of the Ancient Maya (Searchlight Books: What Can We Learn from Early Civilizations?), Matt Doeden (Lerner Classroom, 2015)

Websites

Read theories about why the Mayans disappeared at:
www.bbc.co.uk/history/ancient/cultures/maya_01.shtml

Find out more about the Mayans at:
www.dkfindout.com/uk/history/mayans

Learn more about Mayan life at:
www.mayankids.com

This website has lots of pictures, facts and other information about the Mayans:
http://mexicolore.co.uk/maya

INDEX